The Principles and Practice of

INDIGENOUS CHURCH PLANTING

Charles Brock

BROADMAN PRESS
Nashville, Tennessee

Quotations marked TEV are from the *Good News Bible,* the Bible in Today's English Version. Old Testament: Copyright © American Bible Society 1976; New Testament: Copyright © American Bible Society 1966, 1971, 1976. Used by permission.

Dewey Decimal Classification: 254
Subject heading: NEW CHURCHES
Library of Congress Catalog Card Number: 81-67489
Printed in the United States of America

INTRODUCTION

Over a number of years, Charles Brock demonstrated how to plant many new churches in a semirural area in the northern part of the Philippines. What Charles accomplished there showed the relevancy of church growth principles in the Philippine setting. Charles was able to plant indigenous churches that are today reproducing themselves in the Philippine context. In addition to planting many new units, Charles showed a breadth of vision in relating these churches together in an associational fellowship that has provided a basis for a giving of mutual assistance to each other and for extending the witness of these churches into new and unevangelized areas.

Charles's present assignment is to Manila, an urban area of some ten million people. It is encouraging as well as interesting to see the same principles and practices he utilized in planting churches in the La Union Province of the Philippines is proving successful in the urban setting of Manila as well. This small book is a treasure house of practical wisdom. This has come out of the day-to-day practical experience of a man who is writing not from an ivory tower but out of a daily experience of winning people to Jesus Christ and gathering them into functional churches. I recommend it highly to every missionary who desires to be more effective in winning people and planting churches.

WILLIAM R. WAKEFIELD
Director for South and Southeast Asia
Foreign Mission Board of the Southern Baptist Convention

Foreword

Church planting is an idea whose time has come. It has always been the foundational part of mission work that has been truly effective and has left a lasting contribution. Often the budget, and therefore the priorities, seemed to go to other things.

Today the entire Christian world, almost, is talking about church growth. Conferences are being held at home and abroad about that important, contemporary subject. Some new schools are being started to teach church growth and already established schools are adding it to their curriculum.

More is being written about the fact that we *ought* to plant churches than is being written about *how* to plant churches. Many books are being written to expound a theory of church growth, much of which relates to expanding the size of already existing churches. Not enough of them talk about the process of starting from scratch to plant the congregation in such fashion that it can truly take root in its own soil, find its own identity and reach out in true evangelistic-missionary spirit to its neighbors. This book does precisely that. It is the work of a man who has done the church planting, who is reporting on the work he has done in terms of sound, simple theory that has been proved in action.

Ever since I first read the manuscript I have wanted to see the book made available for wide use. For years I've continued to use in my classes the little book by Melvin Hodges, *The Indigenous Church,* as the most practical book that I could find. In my estimation this book will speak with the same basic, practical approach to today's world and will be very valuable to those who are interested in expanding the Kingdom by the simple New Testament process of helping to plant little churches which testify to the reality of lives changed by the grace of God. I recommend it to you heartily.

R. CAL GUY
Professor of Missions
The Southwestern Baptist Theological Seminary
Fort Worth, Texas

CONTENTS

1

Church Planting—An Overview

The purpose of this book is twofold. The first is to set forth theological and practical church planting principles for feasible indigenous church planting. The second is to give practical suggestions as to how to plant an indigenous church.

A proper theological basis and practical principles of church growth are of major importance to the church planter. An education in various strategies and methodologies is of little value unless there is a corresponding and preceding theology. The greatest need today lies in this area of renewed theological thinking. A proper theology will produce a proper methodology. For the church planter the proper methodology will be natural and inevitable to the degree that it issues strictly from biblical theology.

It is necessary that basic biblical attitudes be internalized into the fabric of the church planter's being before he can have the aptitude to externalize them into action.

Specifically, this relates to the words of Paul, "Let this mind be in you which was in Christ Jesus" (Phil. 2:5). Paul also said in Romans 12:2b, " . . . but let God transform you inwardly by a complete change of your mind" (TEV). Therefore, for the church planter, attitudes precede action; motive precedes motion; organism precedes organization; doctrine precedes doing.

The why of church planting is reflected in biblical theology. A New Testament theology must include church planting and

9

church growth if it is to be complete. Without this Paul's travels and life would have been purposeless. Christ would be de-bodied. The cross of Christ would lose meaning. It was for the church that he died. It was in his death and resurrection that he purposed to create and relate the Body, the church, to the God-head throughout eternity.

Church planting theology and principles involve intense reflec-tive study, but they must also be revolutionary in action. The practical application of church planting principles is the second major purpose of this book. This may be called "finding the handle" in church planting. Not a few missionaries go to their fields of service and end with a frustrating resignation because they could not find the "handle." "Finding the handle" speaks of how to do church planting.

A handle is much more easily found by those who are satisfied to continue the only methods of church planting known to them in the States. This handle is a convenient crutch called money. They learned before coming to the mission field that to plant a church, the first thing to do is buy land, build a building, and develop a church. This is not difficult to do in foreign lands of sparse economies. At least the first two steps are easy—the land and building. The third is more difficult but can be done, and if foreign money and personnel continue to be available the "church" will continue to meet. This method often begins, con-tinues, and ends with a colonial, parental note. For this method-ology the handle is easy to find. However, it will not produce indigenous churches.

But where is the handle if indigenous churches are to be planted? There are two reasons new missionaries are not helped in finding the handle. First, many missionaries do not know how to plant a church apart from heavy foreign aid being infused directly into the new work. Second, new missionaries are not helped in finding the handle because experienced church planters either assume the new missionary knows what to do, or are hesitant to impose their views upon the new missionary for fear of appearing to be presumptuous "know it alls."

Many missionaries have had an introduction to missions in church missions organizations. For the overseas career missionary the education is extended to greater depths in the seminary classroom. Because most seminary curriculums must be broad enough to meet the needs of pastors, educators, and musicians, the emphasis on missions may not be specialized enough to meet basic needs of church planters. It is right that seminary missions classes give weight to the study of missions history, development, and principles of church growth. The seminary may not be the best nor proper place to get down to detailed specifics on how to plant churches, but perhaps some attention should be given to this. This may call for a special class for missionary candidates headed toward a church planting career. This is not to suggest that church planting is the only ministry done by missionaries. But it is so central that everything done on a mission field should be related to it.

The new missionary may be helped to find the handle before his arrival on the field. This can be done in a missionary orientation, a part of which should be much more specific than most general orientation programs. A general orientation concerning culture, language, mission structure, and policies is important, but a more specific orientation directly related to the specific task of church planting would be of great assistance to the church planter. In such an orientation the planter could study and analyze various strategies used in different countries and then give special attention to those strategies used in church planting in his designated country. There should be an introduction to indigenous church planting principles and practice.

A second orientation is of key importance and should come upon the missionary's arrival at his field of service. Often, a mission provides a general hit-and-miss orientation for new missionaries. A typical orientation program may include a meeting with the mission treasurer wherein the treasurer explains the details of financial requisition forms, medical report forms, etc. There is the meeting with the language representative to discuss language learning. In addition to these kinds of training, the missionary needs specific training in what he came to do—plant indigenous churches.

Since the *indigenous church* is the object of the work of the church planter, a clear definition of the term is now in order. It is commonly accepted that an indigenous church is: 1. self-governing; 2. self-supporting; 3. self-propagating. Therefore, an indigenous church administers its own affairs under the Lordship of Christ. Second, an indigenous church provides its own financial support from its members. Third, an indigenous church, out of loving concern, begins other new churches. There is little or no room for flexibility or alteration of these three basic principles. To take away any one of the three makes a church weak, one that falls short of the New Testament pattern.

The indigenous church is a goal and not a method. The goal remains fixed and attainable by various methods. It should be strongly emphasized that certain indigenous methods lead more easily to the goal.

Let us analyze another important term which will be used throughout this book. The term *church planter* is rather new to many people. A church planter is a person, national or foreigner, who sows the gospel seed in such a way that a New Testament church comes to life and grows. Sometimes more general terms are used to describe the missionary such as *field evangelist, evangelist, field missionary,* and *general missionary.* The sad truth is that a field evangelist can be very busy for a full term of four years and never plant a church. *Field evangelist* or *general missionary* often has such a broad meaning that a person can neglect doing the essential of Pauline missionary work (which is church planting) without realizing what's happening. Propping up old work, planning and promoting organizational activity, and serving the mission organization may serve as general outlets of good ministry to the neglect of the highest priority. Watering and cultivating are related to and a necessary part of church planting, but if the missionary does not plant, he may be missing his calling. *Church planter* is a more adequate descriptive term. It is a continual reminder to keep first things first.

Even though church planting is a specialty for some, it is a possibility for many. Using the term *church planter* to zero in on a specific task by specific people does not exclude any other missionary from planting churches. A pastor can and should plant churches. Many businessmen can and should plant churches. Many teachers should plant churches. Churches should plant churches.

This book is designed to encourage and assist the professional church planter and all those other church planters who are such because of the Great Commission.

"Go, then, to all peoples everywhere and make them my disciples; baptize them in the name of the Father, the Son, and the Holy Spirit, and teach them to obey everything I have commanded you. And I will be with you always, to the end of the age" (Matt. 28:19-20, TEV).

2

Theology Produces Methodology

"Your life is shaped by your thoughts" (Prov. 4:23b, TEV). Jesus said, "The mouth speaks what the heart is full of" (Matt. 12:34b, TEV).

Theology is reflected in methodology. A clear understanding of one's theology makes his methodology predictable. The heart of a practical, biblical methodology, or strategy, lies in a biblical theology. For this reason, broad, basic principles precede practice. Practice—actions, strategies, and words—reveal a person's theology whether good or bad, adequate or inadequate.

The resounding conclusion is that a fresh New Testament theology must pervade the life of an indigenous church planter. What one believes about the Bible, salvation, ministry, and the church, as well as other great biblical teachings, is very important. The strategy employed in planting and nurturing a church will depend greatly upon what a person believes. The planter's belief about planting a reproducing church will be reflected in his strategy.

Because a New Testament church is made up of saved people, the planter's view of salvation is of fundamental importance. The church planter has no task unless he believes people without Jesus are eternally lost. Love is the motivating factor in witnessing, yet a real hell is no small factor. A universal humanism falls short in propelling men to bring others to God. Jesus came for a stated purpose—to seek and to save the lost. The planter's task is no less.

Church planting, if extensively done in the Third World nations, must encounter the major world religions. If all Roman Catholics are viewed as Christian, the church planter has little to do in a nation where 85 percent of the people are Roman Catholic. Sometimes a national will ask a missionary, "Why do you come here? We are already Christians." Having the title *Roman Catholic* does not make a person lost, but according to Paul, that person or anyone else is lost if he depends on any other means of salvation than that preached by Paul. This means of salvation is faith in Jesus Christ alone (Gal. 2:16).

While it is important for the church planter to see people as lost if they have not been saved, it is of equal importance for the unsaved to see themselves as lost. A major problem arises in church planting when the planter tries to get people to make "decisions" before they realize they are lost. To try to plant a New Testament church using a typical traditional approach in inviting people to make decisions is often futile. A missionary or an invited crusade evangelist can preach a sound biblical sermon and then ask people to come forward if they believe in Jesus and accept him as their Savior. Many of them will come forward. The problem is that the words used by the planter or evangelist have a completely different meaning for the listener. The listener hears, agrees, and accepts, but he doesn't understand. Those who come forward are often asked typical Southern USA postinvitation questions. Traditional decision cards are filled out by the "new believers." One missionary reported more than one hundred such "decisions" in a crusade. After one year not one of these was ever in attendance at the local church. Some may blame lack of follow-up, but one suspects a greater problem in lack of understanding that everyone must be saved and being saved involves both repentance and faith in Christ as Savior.

Another missionary reports an incident involving the family house girl. She was a lifelong Catholic and had no intention of changing her beliefs. However, for social reasons she attended a Protestant church regularly with her friends. During one service the power of the Holy Spirit was so strong that she found herself responding to the invitation at the close of the service. At the front she was asked to be seated and fill out a decision card. That was all. The young would-be convert responded to a traditionally presumptuous invitation. She was seeking, but she did not find, because a sincere preacher assumed she understood. Seeking, or inquiring, and finding are not synonymous. Seeking is one step, finding is another. The man who asks, "What must I do to be saved?" is not saved until he repents of his sin and trusts Christ as his Savior. The church planter must do his utmost to guarantee, as far as possible, that his seekers understand their lost condition.

If healthy churches are to be planted, the members must have experienced a salvation that includes sanctification. Being saved and sanctified are impossible without repentance. Too often the message of Good News is only partly Good News because it includes faith and surrender, but excludes repentance. This presents a special problem in Asia where there is the cultural fear of "losing face." The cultural conditioning makes it very difficult for a person to say, "I am completely at fault." Before a person can ever be saved he must admit total spiritual failure in his self-efforts. If this point has never been reached, should the church planter then be surprised when many church members continue in their old lives of gambling, lying, and stealing? A theological concept of salvation that takes lightly sin, repentance, and sanctification may produce a religious group but not a true church. "Cheap grace" abounds from fear of hurting feelings and from a desire to be successful. This theology has produced one methodology. A new, more serious theology of salvation will produce a new methodology. Ultimately, each church planter should be led by the Holy Spirit, because it is the Holy Spirit who calls, convicts, saves, and sanctifies. The Spirit has greater freedom to work through the planter who gives heed to the full gospel of salvation.

It would seem reasonable that the practice of a biblical theology regarding salvation would demand slightly altered forms of application. If a planter is preaching on his first night in a community where all the hearers are lifelong Catholics, one question should be asked: In a thirty-minute sermon or Bible study, can the planter have enough input for the unbeliever to repent intelligently and make a genuine surrender? Although many "decisions" would be made if a come-forward invitation were given, it wouldn't be wise to give such an invitation. I believe six to eight hours of intensive Bible study regarding salvation is often necessary before intelligent decisions can be made. The importance of saving faith demands a strategy of prolonged seed sowing (Bible study) if a harvest is to be realized. Many varying ramifications in methodology will be seen when planters believe in the unquestioned necessity of a supernatural experience produced by the work of the Holy Spirit.

Strategy in church planting is strongly influenced and often determined by theological concepts of the basic nature and function of the church. Every serious student of the Bible knows that the New Testament church is made up of baptized believers. These, according to the Scriptures, are the Body of Christ— Christ being the Head.

The fact that in most languages the same word is used to refer to the church and to the place where the church meets has caused a large number of people to confuse the two. This confusion may seem harmless. The problem is that it leads many Christians to think that there can't be a church unless there is a building. You can have one without the other, and it's important to understand this if one is in the work of planting churches. One church expresses this important distinction by saying on its sign "Woodmont Baptist Church Meets Here."

A related difficulty is that many people think that a church is a certain style of building. This kind of thinking can limit a church planter's vision of what can be done in a particular place.

What is the New Testament concept of the church? A church is a group of people, the Body of Christ, who have turned from their sins to place full trust in Jesus as the Christ. They are then baptized. These individuals continue to meet on a regular basis as members of the family of God. They will fellowship in prayer, praise, and Bible study for a definite purpose of glorifying God and furthering his kingdom on earth. The group is a church when gathered and a church when scattered in ministry. This is what the church planter plants. One will note that this abbreviated yet basic definition allows for nurture and growth beyond the birth.

One's theology of ministry will have a powerful impact upon the strategy deployed.

If a person is too professionalized in his concept of ministry, his strategy of church planting and church growth will be different from that of the person who believes in a responsible ministry for every believer. The professionalized person may be characterized by the inability to delegate important responsibilities. He will not find it easy to trust people to do those things which he has been trained to do unless they have been trained as he. He probably prefers to pray publicly, preach, and teach rather than encouraging those of less experience. A church planter with these views will tend toward an overestimation of himself. His method of church planting places great emphasis upon his presence and ability. Usually he practices a direct leadership which is very difficult to reproduce in a new church once he moves to another place.

On the other hand, the church planter can allow every believer to share in the new life adventure of love. This planter believes every Christian has a special ministry. He realizes that every person to whom he ministers is a potential minister. The pastor of a church has the ministry of ministering to ministers.

The planter realizes that even as a young child needs exercise as well as food, so it is with the believer. If the new Christian is provided food but no exercise, he will grow fat and lazy. A new believer may not do a job as well as a professional, but it is only by doing that he will develop his potential as a minister. The church planter with the New Testament concept of ministry thrives more on his knowledge that God is pleased than on the approving applause of followers. Inner security allows the planter to share the limelight even with those of less expertise. He hurts when they stumble and fall and rejoices when they get up and start again. For new believers to realize and fulfill their ministries, the planter must live a life of hurts and rejoicings.

The strategy used will either enhance *the* minister or the *ministers*. The theology held will decide the strategy.

3

Essentials in Church Planting

Dr. Philip Hogan, Executive Director for Foreign Missions of the General Council of the Assemblies of God, urged the three thousand delegates at Lausanne in 1974 to shift emphasis from the human to the divine in world evangelization. In his message he said,

> I am persuaded to believe, that after taking advantage of every tool, pursuing every possible human plan, all one needs to do to find plenty of service is simply to follow the leading of the Holy Spirit. When one engages this truth and begins to live by its principle, there will be whole communities, whole cities, whole nations, whole cultures and whole segments of pagan religions that will suddenly be thrust open to the Gospel Witness . . . Please understand me, I am not pleading for a kind of *"sitting where they sit and letting God happen"* kind of attitude. But what I am pleading for is that at the end of every human endeavor there must be a simple dependence upon the Holy Spirit.[1]

The psalmist says it clearly in Psalm 44:3:

> Your people did not conquer the land with their swords;
> they did not win it by their own power;
> it was by your power and strength;
> by the assurance of your presence,
> which showed that you loved them (TEV).

An absolute dependence upon the work of the Holy Spirit is an indispensable essential in indigenous church planting. No strategy of planting churches is adequate without him. Human wisdom or persuasiveness is of value in church planting only as he is in full control.

That the Holy Spirit opens doors becomes more than a hollow cliché to the Spirit-guided planter. The Holy Spirit uses many ways in directing the planter to fertile fields. He uses circumstances, things, and people, but the planter must always remember the Holy Spirit is essential.

Remembering all Jesus promised that the Holy Spirit would be to the believer (John 16) brings humbled dependence as the planter submits. The planter finds the proper soil to the degree that the Holy Spirit's leadership is followed. As the planter speaks, from the first contact with the people to the day a church is born, the constant working of the Holy Spirit is essential.

Church planting strategy is not a substitute for the leadership of the Holy Spirit. Correct strategy is inspired and governed by the Holy Spirit. The Holy Spirit guides man to the proper strategy and then works through that strategy. A danger faced by all planters is that a strategy may become so methodical that the conscious dependence upon the Spirit fades away. Occasionally every planter should ask himself the question, "What am I daring to attempt that I could not do without the Holy Spirit?" A friend once asked his pastor a thought provoking question. He asked, "If you knew you could not fail, if you threw caution to the wind, if you did not plan around human impossibilities, what would you dare to do for the glory of our Lord?"

Seed sown without the energizing agent of life, the Holy Spirit, lies dormant. He is the one to open the hearts of unbelievers. He is the one to bring conviction of sin. He is the one to bring about conversion and a birth from above. The Holy Spirit is the magnifier and glorifier of the only Hope—Jesus Christ.

The Holy Spirit is essential in church planting after the birth of the church. Often the planter becomes so excited after the birth that he seeks to personally provide for or import people to provide for all the needs of the new church. This limits the planter and the new church in growth. How wonderful to remember that the Holy Spirit lives in new believers. If the church is a product of the Holy Spirit's presence and power, he will give to the members gifts necessary to the life and well-being of the church. This means that the planter can be free to evangelize and plant in another new place. All Christians can be recipients of the gifts of grace freely offered by the Holy Spirit. These gifts of ministry are listed in 1 Corinthians 12.

When a cold theological concept becomes a living personal friend, church planting becomes an unpredictable excitement.

The gospel seed is another essential in indigenous church planting. Paul said, "I have complete confidence in the gospel: it is God's power to save all who believe, first the Jews and also the Gentiles" (Rom. 1:16, TEV). Paul also said, "Christ did not send me to baptize. He sent me to tell the Good News, and to tell it without using the language of human wisdom, in order to make sure that Christ's death on the cross is not robbed of its power (1 Cor. 1:17, TEV).

In nature there is a relationship between the seed sown and the product harvested. The kind of seed sown in church planting is very important if the expected result is to be an indigenous church.

There are many books which may be helpful in introducing people to Jesus, but there is none which can replace the Bible. It was concerning his Holy Word that God said, "So also will be the word that I speak—it will not fail to do what I plan for it; it will do everything I send it to do" (Isa. 55:11, TEV). Only the Scripture can make such a claim as this. The Bible is not magical, but it is miraculous in its source and in its power. The power to penetrate was seen in the postresurrection experience of Jesus and the two men walking from Jerusalem to Emmaus. Note the thing the two men remembered most clearly after Jesus left them. In Luke 24:32, "They said to each other, 'Wasn't it like a fire burning in us when he talked to us on the road and explained the Scriptures to us?' " (TEV). Jesus recognized the Scriptures as essential in revealing truth to the men.

One of the most beautiful experiences of a church planter is to plant the gospel seed day-by-day or week-by-week and see a very obvious change in receptivity and understanding in the lives of the hearers. Gradually the people, by the aid of the Holy Spirit, identify themselves as the sinners for whom Christ died. From the Scripture they learn of their problem and of the solution to that problem. The topical sermon void of much Scripture is not the best tool to use in planting churches. Intellectual exercises to impress the hearers are no more relevant today than they were in Paul's day. The essential is the gospel seed sown in personal simplicity with full trust in God to work his work in the hearers.

Eventually, after the church is born the believers will need to hear and receive the full gospel message with its varied theological ramifications. But in the beginning, before the church is born, before people are born again, what is the essential message?

Unbelievers must understand something of the nature and consequences of sin. Often there is the danger that the unbeliever never gets into the kingdom of God because he never gets out of the rule of sin. Sin and repentance may be watered down for fear of hurting feelings. This is a serious mistake, because Jesus said that without repentance of sin a person could never go to heaven. So a supposed kindness by the planter results in really hurt feelings—after death in hell. Most doctrinal books available for church planting minimize the very first thing an unbeliever must know and accept. The Bible is the best book for church planting because sin is so vividly portrayed.

Another basic biblical truth to be conveyed to the unbelievers is the fact and significance of the coming of God to earth in the flesh to redeem man from the poverty, penalty, and power of sin. For hundreds of years men told of his coming. Much of the New Testament tells of the days when Jesus walked on earth. For Paul, author of nearly half of the New Testament, there is no gospel apart from the cross and the resurrection. The historical how and the eternal why of the crucifixion is an essential part of the gospel seed. The bloodstained cross and the empty tomb make possible the at-one-ment of the believer and God. This was the initial simple seed which Paul sowed in the hearts of unbelievers. Churches sprang up everywhere because he sowed the proper seed and depended on God to bring germination and growth.

The Gospel speaks often concerning man's proper response to the message of the crucified and living Lord. This response may be called "believing," "faith," or "acceptance." This is man's reaction to God's action. God sent; man receives. These truths cannot be taken lightly if the end result is a regenerate church membership. In nations where the Christian religion is popular, it is no big thing for a person to say that he believes in Jesus Christ. The planter cannot be too careful in explaining the biblical concept of repentance and saving faith based exclusively in Jesus Christ. It does make a difference if the foundation members of the newly-planted church are saved and changed.

There is another thing of real importance about the seed sown by the church planter which should be mentioned. There is a large supply of hybrid seed stored in church granaries around the world. Much of it is being planted. This popular hybrid is a mixture of the gospel message and other man-made seeds. This was the principal problem faced by Paul in Galatians. This is usually a mixture of law and grace. Often the hybrid has enough truth to confuse the uncritical mind. Many cults fall into this category. The end result will be affected by the seed sown. If the result is to be a New Testament church, then New Testament seed must be sown in simple, undiluted purity.

Paul sums up the need and content of seed sowing when he says, "Faith comes from hearing the message, and the message comes through preaching Christ" (Rom. 10:17, TEV).

The sower is the third essential in church planting. The role of the sower or planter is seen in Romans 10:14-15 (TEV):

> But how can they call to him for help if they have not believed? And how can they believe if they have not heard the message? And how can they hear if the message is not proclaimed? And how can the message be proclaimed if the messengers are not sent out? As the Scripture says, "How wonderful is the coming of messengers who bring good news!"

All success in church planting depends on the triune Godhead. God the Father is the Grand Designer of the plan of eternal redemption. Jesus the Son is the Redeemer. The Holy Spirit is the Agent of application and sanctification. From beginning to end it is God. But God chose man, when redeemed, to participate in the historical phase of redemption. In previously given Scripture man is thought of as the proclaiming messenger. On another occasion Paul spoke of man as God's ambassador. Other terms to describe this God-ordained work of man in the plan of redemption are: minister, servant, witness, and priest. In the context of this chapter and this book, the sower of the seed is the church planter. It is important to note that the chief church planter of the New Testament was Paul, and he used most of the terms just mentioned to describe his work and his relationship to God's plan of world redemption. There is no question but that the role of sower in church planting is extremely important and even an essential part of God's plan. Perhaps this is what Charles Haddon Spurgeon had in mind when he said, "If God has called you to be a missionary, I'd hate to see you shrivel down to be a king."[2]

The task of the sower of gospel seed is great. To hold in one's possession a message that can set captives free is a staggering responsibility and a glorious privilege. In a sense, the salvation of many people depends upon the sower. If the sower is faithful in his task, many will come to know the Lord and churches will be born. And down through decades of time the lifesaving message of Christ will flow from generation to generation. It started one day when the gospel seed was sown faithfully by the Sower. Seed must be sown before a church can be born, and God has chosen his servants to sow.

The fourth essential in church planting is the soil. Church planting is best done in fertile soil. People who are responsive to the gospel provide a more favorable condition for church planting and church growth than those who are not responsive. It is assumed that a farmer who desires to plant seeds will go to the field. It is a fact that a church planter must be out among the people. He must be aware of who the people are, where pockets of people are located, and something of the religious climate of the area. Churches are not usually planted in a planter's office. The field is the world and the world is people. The gospel seed has never been meant to live apart from people. It came alive historically in a person—Jesus. It spreads through interpersonal relationships when a correct vertical relationship with God has been established. The seed takes on new life and multiplies only as it comes into proper contact with the soil.

The Holy Spirit sends and empowers the sower to sow the gospel seed in the lives of specific, receptive people in order that a new church may be born. When the essentials have their rightful place, churches will be the result.

Notes

1. *Church Growth Bulletin,* January, 1977.
2. A. Clark Scanlon, *Passport to People* (Nashville: Convention Press, 1973), p. vii.

4

Know Your Objectives

A church planter who doesn't know his objectives will walk with the certainty and sense of direction of a blind man. It is important that the planter have some definite measurable goals toward which he is working. The strategy or plan for reaching those goals then must be related to the goals. If the objectives are unclear, then a correct strategy will be unclear or perhaps unknown. Not only should the planter be aware of his objectives, but he should be aware of when one objective is reached and of how to move toward the next objective.

The church planter has more than one objective. His objectives should include: 1. Immediate—the salvation of individuals; 2. Intermediate—the birth of indigenous churches; 3. Ultimate—fellowship of indigenous churches.

The first objective is to lead individuals to saving, transforming faith in Jesus Christ as the only hope of an abundant life. Potential converts must be led to see that their greatest need is greater than food and clothing. If the gospel message is proclaimed clearly, the problem of priorities will take care of itself. Social and economic change will not be the immediate objective of the planter. This will be the natural result when a proper vertical relationship with God is attained. Matthew 6:33 must be preached boldly because Jesus said, "Instead, be concerned above everything else with the Kingdom of God and with what he requires of

29

you, and he will provide you with all these other things" (TEV). Now the church planter must have experiential knowledge of God's protection and care before he can assure the unbelievers that God's promises are true and dependable. Roman Catholic Archbishop Lourdasamy, Associate Secretary of the Sacred Congregation for Evangelism of Peoples, spoke of the danger of losing sight of priorities. He said,

> We should not invest our resources primarily in the economic and cultural development of secular society (with the risk of falling into a sort of clerical paternalization tinged with colonialism), but rather strive to give to mankind, as it gropes for happiness, the imperishable light of the Gospel, which reflects the culture of each country and the personality of each man.[1]

Christ accented the need of man's personal salvation in his preaching and in his death and resurrection. The saving relationship to Christ was central in Paul's preaching and life. He proclaimed that, "If any one is in Christ, he is a new creation; the old has passed away, behold, the new has come" (2 Cor. 5:17, RSV). For Paul, the heart of the mission of the church was reconciling men to God. Paul stated this clearly when he said, "We are ambassadors for Christ, God making His appeal through us. We beseech you on behalf of Christ, be reconciled to God" (2 Cor. 5:20, RSV).

Paul received a clear commission from Christ in Acts 26:18 which tells of the mission of the church: "You are to open their eyes and turn them from the darkness to light and from the power of Satan to God, so that through their faith in me they will have their sins forgiven and receive their place among God's chosen people" (TEV).

Christ began his work with the message, "The right time has come . . . and the Kingdom of God is near! Turn away from your sins and believe the Good News" (Mark 1:15, TEV). At the end of his earthly ministry Jesus said to his disciples, "And in his name the message about repentance and the forgiveness of sins must be preached to all nations, beginning in Jerusalem" (Luke 24:47, TEV).

The first goal, the immediate goal, of the church planter is to lead the unsaved to a meaningful, saving faith in Jesus Christ. There are no worthy secondary or intermediate objectives apart from this foundational objective.

Even though the planter understands the immediate objective, care must be taken to be sure the objective is actually reached. It is easy to get decisions, but difficult to get disciples. This is especially true in countries where being born and baptized in the church means to the people that they are Christian. They often grow up with a reverence for the Bible without a knowledge of its contents. They learn the name of Jesus and accept the historical fact that he is God's Son, but do not know him as the only way to heaven. Therefore, special care must be taken to make the message very clear. For the people with such a cultural and religious background, a typical western "revival" approach may not be the best. This is not to say that some people will not be saved with this approach. Some may be saved as a result of evangelistic crusades, especially if they faithfully attend a series of such meetings.

What is the best way to lead people to a saving knowledge of Jesus? Whether it be a crusade held nightly or a weekly Bible study, prolonged exposure is a key. It is unlikely that one thirty-minute sermon will convince a nominal Christian or a devout pagan to turn from many years of indoctrination. It may take weeks and months before he can understand enough to make an intelligent decision. The ideal is to involve people in a weekly, guided Bible study in which they are exposed to the Bible teachings about sin, repentance, Jesus, his cross and resurrection, and the necessity of man's response in order to be saved. Such a Bible study should give opportunity for a discussion of the above topics. Such a meeting would allow for special sharing of personal salvation testimonies by the leader and special invited guests. Follow-up tracts could be given out after each study. With six to eight hours of such involved study and analysis some people will be ready to become disciples of Jesus.

The Great Commission of Matthew 28:19-20 speaks of making disciples as the immediate objective. Conversion from self-rule to Christ-rule comes before baptism and church family life.

The second major objective of the church planter is to guide the new converts into a family relationship—an indigenous church. It is thoughtless and nonbiblical to lead people to faith in Christ and leave them to develop on their own. It is true that the responsibility of the church planter is to keep moving out to the cutting edge of the work, the unchurched areas. But adequate time must be given to developing indigenous churches. Normally, indigenous churches do not just happen. It is possible that in some places people may be saved and develop into an indigenous church without special guidance by a planter. Usually some guidance is needed. We must remember that the primary work of the church planter is nothing less than church planting.

Philosophies vary on the technique and goal of Bible studies in homes. For the traditional, self-centered church, a Bible study held in a home is never intended to become an indigenous church. Rather, it is an outreach station designed to enhance the big, central church. Often the people come in to the church for worship and the giving of tithes. Maybe this has its place, but it should not be confused with Bible studies held with the definite objective of the development of an indigenous church. If it is only a Bible study to feed the "mother church" it never becomes independent, self-supporting, and self-propagating. Some good may be done, some people saved, and another egg added to the basket for an egocentric pastor. This kind of philosophy of church growth would demand a minimum of churches in a large city. Independent mushrooming of churches would be a threat to the few churches with their controlled Bible studies.

Perhaps the best way to achieve the objective of planting an indigenous church is through personal witnessing and a group Bible study. A serious church planter will have little time for just a Bible study as an end in itself. For each Bible study group the planter has two objectives clearly in mind—salvation of individual members of the group and leading this group toward developing into an indigenous church. This being true, the planter must know what an indigenous church is and the strategy which will most easily lead to the birth of such a church.

The objective is more than planting a church, it is planting an indigenous church. Rarely, if ever, is a strict indigenous strategy of church planting followed. Rarely is a totally indigenous church planted. By indigenous is meant: 1. self-governing; 2. self-supporting; and 3. self-propagating. The church planter must use methods and strategy which will quickly and naturally lead to the establishment of such a church. Every act, every part of the work of the planter, must relate to this objective of beginning an indigenous church. The method of leadership will affect the final objective. The planter's attitude toward the use of money in church planting will affect the end goal. The planter's theology of the nature and function of the church will be reflected in the church planted.

An indigenous church is self-governing. From the beginning of its life the newly-planted church may be influenced by the planter, yet the church will be the one to make necessary decisions at whatever stage of growth it may be. Someone may object and say that the church is too young, uneducated, and inexperienced to make major decisions. The church needs to begin making decisions as it develops. The three-week-old church need not have the knowledge of a ten-year-old church. The planter must be careful to act as a counselor, yet not as a decision maker.

An indigenous church is self-supporting. From the beginning of its life it can and should be so. This means there is no need for outside money to build buildings or finance programs. A new church need not begin at the same level as older churches. It should not try to begin an adult life before it has known childhood. Psychologically, materially, and spiritually the new church is not ready to jump to a full-blown program. In other words, any new church has within its membership money to do all they know how to do properly, and all God calls them to do at that time. So the church planter desires to plant such a church—one which learns to finance its total program through the tithes and offerings of its members. The planter conveys these biblical concepts in his attitudes and practices long before the church is born.

An indigenous church is self-propagating. By its very nature the new church shares its life with others. It will be an evangelistic church. The evangelistic thrust will point to the salvation of individuals and beyond to another new church. If the exploding world population is to be touched significantly with the gospel, new churches must become church-planting agencies. Churches of the New Testament which received, in turn sent out. Every church should be involved in church multiplication. A church begun under indigenous principles will find it easier to reproduce itself than one born out of total support from Christians in another country. Rarely will a church born apart from indigenous principles reproduce itself, and almost never will it produce an indigenous church. It is natural for the child to have the characteristics of the mother. Therefore, for the sake of a lost world, the planter should plant indigenous churches.

The third and ultimate objective of the church planter is a fellowship of indigenous churches. Why such a fellowship? First, it is biblical. A casual reading of the New Testament reveals that there was a special relationship among the churches. There was also a special relationship among the leaders of the various churches. There was advice, counsel, and material sharing seen in that special relationship. Members visited from church to church for reasons of encouragement, teaching, preaching, correction, and mutual sharing.

Such a relationship is needed today for the same reasons as in Paul's day. Encouragement is often the first need which can be met through a fellowship among churches. This is especially true in areas where the new believers face persecution. It is not uncommon for believers to face family and economic excommunication because of their new religion. Often, it is glue such as this that initially binds the local church together as a family. If there is another group of people down the road facing the same persecution, fellowship becomes natural for the two groups.

Another reason for fellowship is sharing the joy of the newly-found Savior. There is also benefit in sharing problems and victories. Eventually, the churches benefit by sharing mutual projects, some of which may be impossible to accomplish by one new church.

If the planter has helped in the planting of several churches in the same area, he would be the logical person to encourage each church to get to know the other churches of like faith. The planter could suggest a special fellowship meeting with all the churches invited. Once the churches meet for a fellowship of sharing, praise, and study, they likely will be excited about meeting again. Soon, quarterly or monthly meetings may be desirable. The emphasis should be on an informal, voluntary fellowship. There is no need to structure the fellowship after any pattern followed in other areas of the nation or world. It should be organized only as much as necessary to meet the needs and purposes of the churches involved. This may be simply called a fellowship or association of churches. The traditional use of the term *association* has often resulted in a lot of political ladder climbing with a heavy emphasis on business, but little fellowship. If the churches are indigenous and New Testament, a fellowship is natural.

Even though the planter should lead the churches to get to know each other, he should also be aware of certain dangers. As has been stated, there is the natural tendency toward a power structure which supersedes the local church. Never should any organizational structure evolve that takes away the self-rule of the local church. Each church is totally independent under the Lordship of Jesus Christ. So whatever relationship may be established among churches, that relationship should never govern the individual churches making up the relationship. While there are potential problems in these fellowships, the potential benefits outweigh the problems.

Another danger akin to the power structure is the danger of personal power struggles within the fellowship of churches. A correct healthy emphasis on the brotherhood of all believers from the very beginning will help. A motto such as "Everybody is somebody" believed in the hearts of every member will lessen this danger of power struggles.

The church planter need not be closely related to the churches and to the fellowship of churches indefinitely. He should not settle in as boss with no thought of going to unchurched areas. If the churches are strong, they themselves can plant new churches in their immediate area.

It may be helpful if the fellowship of churches will choose one from their group to serve as area missionary. His work would be to assist the existing churches in special needs and to lead in further penetration of the area with church planting.

The original planter is then free to go to new regions to start over again. He can say with Paul, "My ambition has always been to proclaim the Good News in places where Christ has not been heard of" (Rom. 15:20, TEV). As he goes to the new region he will work toward reaching the same three objectives: 1. the salvation of individuals; 2. the establishment of indigenous churches; and 3. the leading of churches into an indigenous fellowship.

Note

1. *Church Growth Bulletin,* January, 1972, p. 193.

5

Speaking the Language of the People

Speaking the language of the people is of primary importance to the church planter. Learning the dialect is essential for maximum efficiency in church planting. (Planters struggling with the dialect may consider it of minimal importance.) There is another area of importance in communicating effectively which goes beyond the dialect. It is possible to be fluent in a dialect yet never speak the "language" of the people.

Learning the dialect is an important part of church planting. This is the place where many missionary church planters begin to stumble. There are difficulties in learning a new language. This is especially true for most Americans. Americans normally have no need to learn two languages. English is their language. The average American doesn't often meet a person who cannot communicate with him in English. He can even travel to many other countries and still get by in English. College education often will include the study of a foreign language, but generally this is purely academic. Most of the students never expect to rely on their knowledge of the foreign language in a living situation. Most Americans seem to have a subconscious attitude that anyone who wants to communicate with them can learn their language —English.

Physiological and psychological strain are inherent in learning a new language. It is physically exhausting to concentrate on a strange language. There is a mysterious draining of one culture and the infusion of a new culture, to the point of sharing in two cultures. Language and culture are so intertwined that to have one means sharing in the other to some degree. A living, daily use of a new language means giving up some of the old culture and an accepting of some of the new culture. Physically and psychologically this will have unspoken deep effects.

The church planter then needs to understand why he should learn the dialect of the people to whom he wishes to minister. A person's native tongue is his heart language—the language of his emotions. When he is confronted with something so intimate as the life-changing gospel of Jesus Christ, he needs to hear it in his heart language so that it can permeate every part of his understanding and being. Remember that one of the miracles on the Day of Pentecost, as recorded in Acts, was that as the apostles preached, every man heard in his own language. This was necessary for maximum understanding.

If a person does not hear the gospel message in his native tongue he is not only limited in his own understanding, he is seriously limited in being able to in turn relate that message to others. If the people use their native dialect in normal living, then revert to a foreign language to convey spiritual truths, these truths come across as foreign and unnatural. When God calls out leaders from among the new believers, it is a serious hindrance to their ministries if they must receive their training in a foreign language.

A part of the planter's need to learn the language involves more than words. A missionary's attitudes toward personal involvement in learning the language speak louder than words. One of the chief ways to communicate love is to learn to speak the language of the people. When a national sees a foreigner labor over learning the language, it makes a good impression. If a missionary never tries to learn to speak to the national in the native tongue, the national may feel that he is unimportant as far as the foreigner is concerned. A missionary may object, and say, "The nationals are more impressed with good English than a mistake-filled, stumbling use of the native dialect." This is an excuse and will be made only by someone who does not want to learn the language. Anyone who seriously desires to minister to the real needs of people must learn to speak the heart language of the people. Every foreign missionary who is willing to invest a lifetime in a foreign land should strive diligently to learn the language of those people to whom he will minister.

What about the church planter who just cannot learn the language? A reputed linguistic expert recently told a group of missionaries that a missionary who cannot learn enough basic language to get by in a culture should be sent home. This would be especially true of church planters. The planter must be among the people in times of joy and crisis. He must speak the language of the people if he is to be effective. It is an insult to the intelligence of the planter and to the value of the nationals for a church planter to be forced to have a companion as interpreter wherever he goes. Every church planter who is intelligent enough to go to a foreign land as a missionary is capable of learning a new language.

Motivation is the key. Language programs may serve as avenues of learning a language, but the personal motive is of greater importance. If a person wants to badly enough, he will. The motive for the church planter is no less than a personal commission from God to communicate a lifesaving message to spiritually dying people. The love of God, the love for God, and the love for lost people will drive the church planter to learn the emotional, heart language of the people he seeks to win.

Effective communication involves more than learning the native dialect. Some may know the dialect and never speak the "language" of the people. Beyond dialect lies cultural understanding and adaptation—the emotional and mental compatibility. This applies to church planting in one's homeland as well as in a foreign land. Regional cultural differences demand a new understanding and adjustment. The city person may have difficulty in speaking the language of the rural people. The highly educated may also have problems in speaking the language of the less educated. By "speaking the language" in this context is meant the ability to relate to another person.

In a day of rising nationalistic spirits in all nations and especially among the Third World nations, there is a waning welcome to superior-minded missionaries—too superior in their own minds to identify with or relate to the people. There is demand for missionaries who can relate on a level of mutual respect.

Does this mean that the church planter is to give up his own nationality? No, he cannot do this and perhaps will do more harm than good if he tries. In a recent lecture, an anthropologist from the University of the Philippines told of an extreme case of seeking to identify. A well-intentioned foreign missionary went to minister to a tribal people in northern Philippines. He wanted to really "speak the language of the people." He secured the scanty one-piece garment common to those people and a spear, and proceeded to walk through the village wearing those two items and nothing more. That was a real identity crisis! The people did not respect him. He overidentified and soon left the country. Of course, this is an unnecessary extreme.

A word of warning may be needed here for the American missionary church planter who has a family and lives away from other missionary families. If the family loses its American identity in its quest for identifying with the new culture, there may be real problems ahead for the children. The child must not be allowed to lose his own identity in order to fit into the culture. No matter how hard he tries to be like those around him, he is still different. He will only become frustrated that he cannot be just as they are. Also the time will come when he must return to live among American people. He may find that he doesn't fit in with that culture either. He has lost his identity. He isn't sure who he is, American or other, and consequently is not sure what to do or how to act. As he goes back to the States for college, insecurity from a displaced identity may cause him to be more susceptible to social problems. A church planter, in his effort to relate to a new culture, cannot and should not cease to be an American.

The planter must, however, avoid the other extreme. To be an American in every way on every day is failure to recognize the context as it is. The American is an American, but he is also relating to people who are not American. Only a superior attitude would insist that the national bend to the American's cultural demands. Most nationals would expect Americans to live somewhat the way Americans live. There should be a commonsense Christian stewardship level of living which, when possible, permits the American to live as an American, yet not like a king. The planter should not seek to live on a level that puts him beyond the ordinary people. Simplicity in living style will be an asset to the church planter.

It is neither realistic nor practical for a foreigner to seek to totally become like one of another nationality. There can be redemptive relationships with respect from both parties, the national and the foreigner, without the foreigner going to either extreme of overidentification or withdrawal from cultural contact.

Our chief example of "learning the language"—of identification with others—is the coming of Christ to a foreign land to meet the needs of people. He became one of the human race in order to bring man to God. He identified with man and his needs. He was sent by the Father to perform a mission among men. He partook of life as he found it. He worked, ate, suffered, was tempted, was disappointed. He wept.

The missionary too must go among men, speak their language, and relate to their life. He must immerse himself in the culture of those he hopes to win. He can only bring about spiritual change as he is able to relate to people. The planter must live within the culture of those to whom he is ministering. He must adapt to new ways. His mission is not to change culture. His mission is to lead people to Christ who will change hearts, which in turn will influence culture.

Acculturation is only a part of the church planter's learning to speak the language of the people. There are important peculiarities in all nations, but the planter must understand that there are some basic universal similarities among all people. One of these similarities is that all people are searching for inner peace. Only as the church planter is aware of this can he redemptively relate to the people.

Another similarity common to all men is a desire for reality. When the planter practices an open, honest life he is more able to relate to other people. When he is able to show his humanness, other real humans will understand his language. They will relate. To reveal a total person, one who doubts, fears, becomes discouraged, who knows joy and peace, ups and downs, will open the doors to an international language beyond dialect which is understood by all.

The fright and fear of death is a part of all people without Christ. The guilt of sin is spelled the same way in all languages.

Release from guilt is a universal quest. Knowledge of these truths enables the missionary, who himself has experienced all these fears, guilts, and thirst for peace, to relate to the needs of others. He knows the heart language of the people. He must share the message of hope heart-to-heart, in simple clarity, so the people will understand.

Every church planter must learn the dialect. Beyond that he must identify with fallen humanity in the midst of their culture and in word and deed lead them to God.

6

Meeting the People
Where They Are and Leading
Them to Dignity and Freedom

Twenty years ago a missionary in Missouri made a statement which a young pastor never forgot. Gerald Locke was speaking to a young church when he announced his goal for a series of preaching services. He said, "We are here to lead you from where you are to where God wants you to be."

This statement recognizes that the missionary must know where people are in their needs. It also says that the missionary must go near the people in their position of need. There is the ring of tenderness, of patience, like a shepherd caring for wayward sheep. There is understanding and sympathy for the person who needs to be led to God's way. This statement also assumes that the missionary leader understands the God-acceptable position to which he is leading the wayward. Two of the major characteristics of the God-acceptable position are dignity and freedom.

People must be met where they are—*in their native context of thought.*

"Native" refers to the natural—that in which and with which people are born and reared. Some people claim that the Christian has no business pushing his religion upon non-Christian societies. They say, "They have their religion, leave them alone." The answer to this is that the core of Christianity, unlike other religions, is others-centeredness. The Christian message of hope serves as a magnet to draw those whose lives have been brought to despair by the blinding blight of bondage to sin. In many cases, even the forms of other religions have deepened the depths of hopelessness. The very nature of Christianity is revolutionary, changing attitudes and lives wherever it goes. Where there is bondage, the antidote is the key of release found in Jesus. The church planter must deliver the Christian message in the native context of thought.

The church planter goes to people who have thoughts and philosophies strange and different from his. He does not go to condemn or to condone. He goes with a strong positive message centered in God's Word. The Holy Spirit, in his own good time, will use the Scripture to bring about judgment, conviction, correction, and conversion. The task of the planter is not to do these things which God has foreordained to be the work of the Holy Spirit.

An example of this is seen in an experience of a missionary who went to a small community chapel, upon the invitation of the people, to lead them in Bible study. The people were nominal Christians but had a strong desire to study the Bible. The first night the front was lined with burning candles. At the beginning of the meeting the people politely asked the missionary if they could say their prayers. Should the missionary have told them no? The people went to the front and said their prayers. As the missionary sat near the front, the leading man in the community said, "Do you see that hole over there?" There was an earthen platform at the front of the chapel. At the base of the platform was a small hole the size of a baseball. It resembled a drain hole. Below the hole was a six-inch sunken area the size of a single bed. In the sunken area bamboo strips had been tied together for people to lie on as they looked into the hole. The man continued, "Every night people look into that hole. Sometimes they see fire, stars, the moon, and if lucky they see Jesus with a long, flowing beard. Sometimes they smell the ointment Mary used on Jesus two thousand years ago." The missionary had a doubt about all this. Apparently the man saw this doubt for he said, "Here, smell this." From his pocket he brought a small brown bottle. "One night when the odor was very strong, we took this dirt from the hole and put it into this bottle. Here, smell," he said. The missionary smelled. There was an odor, a sweet one. The native context of thought was apparent.

What was the church planter to do? What would have been the result if the planter had openly said no to the people when they wanted to pray? What if he had said a strong no to the people concerning the fragrant soil? He could have openly condemned the people and the practices. This would also have closed the door before any gospel seed could be planted.

The Gospel seed was planted week after week. The superstitious prayers stopped and the candles disappeared as the Holy Spirit enlightened the thoughts of the people. People stopped searching for Jesus in the hole when they found him in the Word. Within two months twenty-four adults received Christ and were baptized. After five years this church still continues to grow in their new context of thought.

Remember that the answer is not condoning or giving approval to all the native thought, leaving the people where they are. Rather, it is to take them where they are, patiently lead them into the light of God's Word, and trust the Holy Spirit to bring enlightenment and conviction. The people will know where the planter stands without the planter condemning them.

Pagan practices and beliefs are very real to the people. There are supernatural beings and powers which are not of God nor from God, but they are real. The planter need not deny reality. Such things are found in the Bible. Condemned and ungodly, but biblical, historical fact they are. Unless the church planter meets the people where they are, in the normal, natural setting of their thoughts, he can never lead them away from those thoughts. The starting place for the people is where they are. This is the beginning of the journey toward a new dignity and freedom brought about by the indwelling Christ.

People must be met where they are *in the native context of things.*

The planter should go to the natural, physical setting of the people and plant seed there. This is where the people live most of their hours. This will be the normal context of the living out of their new-found life. There is no need to segregate the day-to-day living from their newly-found religion. If the new faith is valid, it can and will live and prosper in the native context of things, the native neighborhood or community. It may be harmful to build a new Western-style chapel away from the people's natural setting and then try to convince them to go to the chapel to learn about Jesus. There are a number of hidden dangers in this approach. First, few will come unless offered prizes or free joy rides. A second danger is that many of the people may assume that Jesus is either Western or upper-middle class if one must go to such a place to find him. The third danger is the removal of the sacred from the natural, secular context of life. The fourth danger is the difficulty of reaching many of the people where they live if the meeting place is too far from and different from the native context of things.

The church planter meets the people where they are in their native *thoughts* and leads them to where God wants them. Only a part of this statement is necessarily true regarding meeting people where they are in the native context of *things.* He meets them where they are and ministers to them where they are, but does not necessarily lead them to forsake the natural physical and material ways of living. While certain sinful practices will cease when Christ comes in, a person may continue to worship by the aid of an oil light. The people living in grass huts may also worship God in grass huts. People who live in high-rise apartments may also worship God in high-rise apartments. The slum dweller may also worship God in the slum setting. The primary concern of the church planter is not social betterment, economical adjustments, or political change. He meets the people in their native context in these areas and plants the revolutionary gospel seed, allowing it to make changes as it will.

Planting churches in the native context of things will lead away from the concept of one big-town church designed for all the people to attend. This is necessary if the population is to be penetrated with the gospel. In many nations there should be an evangelical church congregating within easy walking distance of all people in the cities and communities. If this were true, churches would often be found meeting in homes of members, in rented halls, or other facilities in the natural setting. In order to do this, the planter must have a biblical concept of the church and ministry. Egocentric fear of competition of having another church too close would have no place in this system of church growth. The aim is to reach the people with the gospel message, and this is best done in the native context or natural setting of the people.

The church planter has definite objectives in mind. He knows where the people are, and he knows where they should be led to. When the planter first meets the people without Christ, they are in bondage to sin. They are slaves of sin. From this life of slavery and bondage where are the people to be led? They should be led to a new life in Christ, characterized by a newfound dignity and freedom.

Paul desired these qualities of dignity and freedom for the Galatian believers, but they faced temptations to follow paths which led back to bondage. There were people who tried to lead the Galatians to a dependence upon circumcision even after they began their new life by faith. The Galatians were already freed by faith in Christ alone, yet they were tempted to become slaves again.

Today the same temptations are present in various forms. The church planter points the unbelievers to Christ and leads them to accept Christ as Savior and Lord. Much depends upon the church planter in where the final dependency of the people will rest. It is possible that the planter will start right with full dependency on Christ as the Head and then gradually permit the people to return to a dependency upon the planter. Symptoms of this human-based dependency appear when the believers begin to think of the planter as someone other than a brother. They may desire to give him a superior title. It is seen when people cease to initiate projects or programs unless they have the approval of the church planter. The people begin to clear everything with the planter. Some begin to think of him as boss. These are unhealthy signs indicating too much dependence on humanity. From the beginning, a church should employ a strategy which will encourage a continuing dependency upon Christ.

The church planter may know what is right. He may know the ideal toward which he will lead the people. Yet there is a subtle temptation for the natural man in the planter to gain control and permit, and sometimes encourage, the people to depend upon him. This can be an unparalleled ego trip for the planter. At the same time it will destroy the potential of the believers. There is neither dignity nor freedom to be found in reliance upon a church planter.

The wrong use of money is a major factor in creating dependency on the planter, which in turn dilutes the dignity and stifles the freedom of the new believers. One does not need to be on a foreign mission field long before he sees cripples produced by the attitude that money solves all problems. Money is usually a greater hindrance than help in producing indigenous churches. In some nations it is rare to find an indigenous church where the congregation was first given land, building, and a salaried pastor. This creates a dependency from which freedom is absent and often not even wanted because no true self-respect and sense of dignity has been created in the believers.

True love frees a person to be somebody of importance as he is linked to the only source of real life, Jesus. There is no greater area of needed discipline than in the expression of redemptive love. Often a disciplined, redemptive love must say no to the wants and even to the temporal needs of people if eternal needs are to be met. In many of the developing nations the flashing of a dollar forever damages the potential spiritual vision of the unbelievers. The end result will be a group of national churches which cannot or will not attempt any important project of outreach or education unless someone outside helps them. How many missionaries have heard the sickly echo, "What will the mission do to help?" The sickness is kindled by missionaries who in "love" say, "We will do it for you."

Dignity and freedom lie along the path of New Testament indigenous churches. Planters must want this for the new believers. This kind of dignity and freedom in Christ releases the churches to be creative and daring. The presence of the church planter would be an asset, but without him the churches would go on without missing a step. Their head is Christ; the Bible is their manual of instruction and action; the church is his body. This concept makes the term *supervisor* a little out of place for the church planter.

The Liberator, the One who sets captives free and sustains them in their walk, is the Holy Spirit. This fact relieves the planter of a burden too heavy for any man to carry. It also brings humility to the planter who knows that he is dependent upon another for all wisdom and power. This person is the Holy Spirit. It is he who gives the gifts to do anything worthwhile.

The Holy Spirit gives new life to the dead through making Christ alive in their hearts. It is a joy to observe changed attitudes and receptivity brought about by the Holy Spirit. When a group of people are saved, the Holy Spirit works in their hearts to lead them into fellowship with each other. The church is formed with Christ as Head. The Holy Spirit lives in the hearts of the believers to guide the believers individually and as a group. The Holy Spirit may use the church planter as an instrument of ministry, but the key to growth is the One, the Holy Spirit, who lives in their hearts every day. The church planter's primary concern is not the success or failure of the newborn church, but his position in the program of the Holy Spirit. Through all the liberating and the sustaining, the Holy Spirit is the Agent of Change, and Christ is the only One to be exalted and glorified.

The church planter meets the people where they are in their native context of thought and things, and through the power of the Holy Spirit, leads them to a new dignity and freedom in Jesus Christ.

7

"Thinking Reproducible" in Every Aspect from Beginning to End

One of the three major characteristics of an indigenous church is its ability in Christ's strength to reproduce itself. This has been called self-propagation. A church does not attain this characteristic easily nor by accident. The way a church is born will influence its ability to reproduce itself. A church planter cannot be sure every church he plants will actually begin new churches, but he can do everything possible to leave the way open for such a self-reproducing church.

A church's view of reproduction will be learned early. Every action of the church planter becomes part of a lesson learned by the church, even during its birth. The planter's relationship to the church can be likened to a parent-child relationship. The child is learning from every action of the parent even though the parent isn't consciously teaching and the child isn't consciously learning. (Sometimes through his actions the parent teaches the child things he never intended to.) If the church planter is fully aware of the need for "thinking reproducible" in everything done, he will more likely plant a church capable of reproduction.

In an age when perhaps more than three billion people do not know Christ, it may be a shortsighted stewardship for a church ever to be born without a definite idea of reproducing itself. The birth of new churches is God's chosen way of spreading the Good News to all people. God does not will that people be born again without becoming a part of a local congregation of believers. Therefore, when people are saved, God has determined that they enter a new family. This family, the church, provides nourishment and needed love for maturation of the members. Churches that produce new churches are a necessity; it is God's will. If this is an accepted fact, the church planter must think reproducible in every aspect of planting a church, from the time the first seed is sown to the actual birth of the church and as it continues to grow.

In planting a reproducible church, the planter must always "think reproducible"—*in the use of material things.*

The strategy the church planter uses concerning material things must be tailored to the economy of the local area. It must be possible for the local church, once it is born, to reproduce itself. The planter should not use anything which the people cannot provide for themselves. The planter is always teaching unspoken lessons concerning church planting. What kind of reproducible example is he using when he goes to an area where there is no electricity and uses a special gadget attached to his automobile to produce current? From this current he can have lights, use a public address system, play recorded music, or even show movies. He has unconsciously taught the people that these things are necessary. Long before the new church thinks of reproducing itself in another place, it must decide how to continue and how to attract and feed the people without the things used by the church planter. The church members will be tempted to give up because they can't do it like the planter did. The material "crutches" used by the missionary appeared to be a blessing, but stymied, stunted, irreproducible growth becomes a tragedy.

What about using movies in church planting? Movies will gather a crowd almost anywhere. But "think reproducible." After the people are saved, become a church, and think of planting a new church, where do they get the movies? The planter has taught a lesson he cannot easily unteach.

What musical instruments should be used in church planting? It depends on the people. If an accordion is easily within their means and readily available there will be no harm in the planter using an accordion. There are some places where a guitar is best, because even very poor people can afford such an instrument. To carry expensive electronic equipment and public-address systems into low economy areas is not "thinking reproducible." It is easy to get crowds when using entertainment props and mechanisms, but few true disciples come from this. This is not to speak against good music and well-presented programs. It is speaking for a sensitivity to the reproductive capabilities of the local economy. Everything used by the planter should be within the power of the people's economy to provide.

It is healthy to let the people provide all the physical necessities from the beginning. The planter should take himself, his gospel seed, and little else. The people will provide a place, seating, lights, etc., if the planter expects them to. An example of this is seen in the practice of one church planter who has planted several churches with the people reading by small oil lights. The church planter could have carried a gas lantern to be used by the people, but preferred the native context of things which the people could provide in his absence. If he takes his lantern every time, what will the people do when he must be absent? They cannot meet because they don't have the light. There is the danger of a growing dependency that will create a situation quite difficult to reproduce if there is no planter present.

Material things, such as lights, public-address systems, movies, and even church houses, are not essentials in church planting.

Remember that the essentials are the Holy Spirit, the seed (Bible), the soil (people), and the sower (church planter). The planter should give much thought before using material objects. Some are helpful. Some, if used as a crutch or to entertain, are foreign to New Testament church planting. The planter may provide and use these crutches with the idea that later they will be given to the people for their use. But if the people cannot afford items which are used and finally given to them by the church planter, chances are they cannot afford to maintain and care for them.

From the first day, the first contact with the people, "think reproducible." Do not use anything which the people cannot or will not provide for themselves. Stingy? No! A growth producing stewardship? Yes. Such growth is desirable wherein independent self-hood is realized with full dependence upon Christ.

The church planter should "think reproducible"—*in every detail of strategy used.*

Normally, he should not do anything which the people cannot do themselves shortly after they are saved. Strategy involves the plan of action used in planting the church. From the first contact with the people the planter is following a strategy, planned and unplanned.

The strategy should fit into the local cultural framework to allow the local residents to comfortably reproduce a church. If the church planter uses a strategy foreign to cultural acceptance, he may be partially successful in planting a church, but he has made it very difficult for that church to plant another church.

What strategies are most easily reproduced?

General strategies vary from country to country and from missionary to missionary. There is not one strategy that should always be used to the exclusion of all others. When he is "thinking reproducible" the planter may find some strategies of penetrating a community for the purpose of church planting may have precedence over others. The total culture will be a partially determining factor in the technique or strategy most successful and reproducible. Within the culture the economy is a factor worth studying. Also, the religion of the people will influence the method of penetration to be chosen. The kind of religion and the popularity of the religion among the people are factors which influence strategy.

The use of evangelistic crusades is a popular strategy for many church planters. When such crusades are used, there usually is a need for special follow-up evangelistic classes. These must be followed with classes for new believers. Though the crusade plan has proven valuable in many areas, the question of reproducibility still should be answered. In some countries church planting has employed the use of great mass crusades led by a foreigner to the extent that reproducibility by a local newborn church is impossible. Many times crusades are too expensive for the local church to reproduce. The image of a successful crusade may be so high in the quality of leadership and program that a small local group could never duplicate it. There are other problems built into mass crusades as a church planting strategy. A major problem exists for highly trained, persuasive evangelistic crusaders. They may go to an area in a developing nation where independent, democratic action is a foreign behavior. In an effort to please, to open avenues of financial security, to follow the crowd, many new "converts" will make decisions. A few of these may be genuine, but many will not be. The Christian faith is still an affair between God and the individual. A degree of understanding is necessary before a real conversion is likely. The message of many mass meetings hits the crowd with a glancing blow, never becoming a personal encounter for most individuals.

Mass meetings may be useful in church planting, but they should be reproducible on a local level by the local people. This means that church planting crusades are best done on a lower key by local people. A national pastor or missionary is to be preferred over the nonoriented, nonacculturated foreigner. These are leaders who know the people, their needs, and heart language. Once a new church is planted using this strategy, it is within the realm of possibility that the church can plant another church.

Consider a general statement: The greater the nationalization from the beginning of a church planting project, the more likely the planted church will be a reproducing church. This means leadership by local people at their own level of ability and understanding, administering their chosen program to speak to the people in their language and culture. This is reproducible in any society.

A major strategy which is most practical, effective, and usable is the popular community Bible study. This is a program with a star personality—Jesus Christ. This is a program with a universal manual—the Bible. This is a program designed for all people. The way of salvation is made clear. Reproductivity is the natural outworking of the indwelling Christ. A disciple of the Lord without extensive formal training can guide such a study of God's Word and permit the Holy Spirit to be the Teacher. Church planting using this strategy is not limited to foreign personnel, foreign capital and gadgets, or college and seminary graduates. It is unlimited because it is reproducible by the local church.

If the church is to reproduce itself, the planter must use a church planting strategy intellectually acceptable to the people. The strategy must be on the people's level of understanding.

There is one general standard to follow among the highly educated or the uneducated. Simplicity has a beauty appreciated by all who are searching for God. The strategy should be within the mental grasp of anyone who desires to plant a new church.

Everything a church planter does is important because it is a part of an overall strategy which will either find its end in the birth of a church, or it will produce a reproducing church.

A church planter should think "reproducible"—*in the kind of leadership used.*

A good leader uses transferrable leadership methods. Only the planter who plans to stay in a new church for many years can settle into a permanent position of leadership. If his goal is shared leadership responsibilities, he is free to plant more churches. He also frees God-given gifts in people in the newborn church.

It has been stated that the planter should not take anything to the people or practice any strategy which the people cannot reproduce. This is just as true in leadership methods. Everything the planter does in teaching, praying, and singing should be reproducible by the group shortly following salvation and baptism. Much more will be said concerning this in a later chapter.

There is beauty and an excitement of accomplishment in thinking and practicing reproducible principles. There is a great sense of fulfillment in seeing a newborn church become strong enough to stand alone. Practicing reproducibles in the use of things, strategy employed, and leadership methods will often lead to such a church, a church that is not only self-governing and self-supporting, but also self-reproducing.

8

Getting Started

Attention should now be focused on "how to do it" or "finding the handle" in indigenous church planting. First, it must be understood that there are some constants in church planting. These have been dealt with in previous chapters. These have to do with essentials necessary and the theological foundations for indigenous church planting. These will not vary. In every nation, educated or not, urban or rural, basic principles remain the same.

A great deal is being written about philosophy and principles of indigenous church planting. There is a shortage of material from the church planter's perspective about the mechanics of church planting. Some well-intentioned missionaries go to a foreign land to plant churches and end up in a frustrating resignation because they were never able to find the handle in church planting. Others may spend years looking for the handle. Church planting is a foreign concept to most stateside pastors and leaders, especially church planting in areas where there are no Christians to begin with. Thus, there is no background experience to acquaint the new church planter with church planting techniques. Some of this could be done in orientation before going to the mission field and a wise on-the-field orientation will go beyond general philosophy, budgets, houses, cars, and policies. At least one technique of planting churches should be clearly explained and perhaps demonstrated for the new church planter.

Getting a handle will be the chief concern of these closing chapters. Be it understood that theology is constant; methodology varies. Though a technique will be suggested in these pages, it does not assume that this is the only valuable technique used by church planters, including the author.

Some of the suggestions may appear to be very simple, but experience and testing lie behind every detail. The small, seemingly "everybody knows that" things are significant parts of a total strategy. At a church planting clinic a church planter was sharing a technique for planting churches. At the end a leading pastor stood up and said, "We have known these things all the time. There is nothing new here." In response another stood up and said, "Yes, we have known and it is not new, but we have not done it." The problem is not knowing philosophically and giving mental assent. The problem is how to apply what is known. Perhaps it should be stated here that indigenous church planting cannot be learned in a classroom, and especially from a teacher who has never planted an indigenous church. A philosophy may be learned in the classroom, but not a living practical knowledge. Church planting is caught more than taught.

The approach and technique to be considered here is biblical. It is universally possible, and it is reproducible in any culture and economy, with local leadership. Before looking more closely at this Bible study method, note some practical pointers necessary to be understood before actually teaching the Bible.

Who can plant a church? Again, it may be necessary to remember what kind of church is to be planted. If it is a traditional American church with all its trappings, the planting will be limited to Americans or Americanized nationals. In some countries this is the standard objective in church planting. This is shown in many ways. An annual request for statistical reports from church planters prompted one missionary to write on the request form, "Is this from Nashville or from our country?" Such Westernized questionnaires indicate the kind of churches generally planted. Few nationals could do it, and most would not if left to their own resources. The number of planters who can plant this kind of church is highly limited.

In order to open the door for wide participation in church planting, a New Testament view of the church is necessary. Nothing less and nothing more than the New Testament pattern is needed. This releases the church planter who has no money for land or buildings, hospitals, and schools. This releases a farmer to plant a new church. No! You don't have to be "ordained" to plant a church. Nor is the assistance and advice of such a person essential. A business man can start a new church. Winston Crawley of the Southern Baptist Foreign Mission Board made an interesting statement in a monthly missionary newsletter. He said,

> We have to get away from the feeling that the preacher must do it all, and that we can't carry on a worthy program unless he has been to Seminary. How subtle it is—this idea that everything centers in a building and in a seminary-trained leader, and unless you have those two evangelism can't go forward. . . . I doubt that you will find that subtle idea in the New Testament. Some way we must break away from this pattern.[1]

If the world is to be influenced significantly, church planting must become a live option for more people. A quick reading of Romans 16 will suggest that many people were involved in church planting. Paul was used mightily of God and was a great church planter, but where would he have been without Priscilla and Aquilla, Ampliatus, Urbanus, Apelles, Rufus, Gaius, and others? Like an overflowing stream, the common believers, pushed out by persecution, pushed out from province to province, went to other people to plant the seed from which would spring new fellowships of believers—churches (Acts 8).

Young people can plant churches. No, not extension Bible classes, or home Bible classes, but real, live, indigenous churches. One Bible school is now sending out six teams of young people one day each week. Their objective is planting indigenous churches. Some older missionaries who have observed their program have been amazed at how God is using these young people. Youth can plant churches. The author of this book, now serving as a church planter in a foreign country, planted his first church when eighteen years of age. (Yes, without a sponsoring mother church or salary.)

Who can plant churches? Anyone who, under the leadership of the Holy Spirit, really desires to. There is a call, a gift bestowed upon those who desire to plant churches. The call may come first with the gift bestowed and developed as it is used. The point of these paragraphs is that man's standards and God's standards as to who can plant a church often are far apart. Many say few are qualified; God says that his gift is the chief qualifying factor in who can plant churches.

First Corinthians 1:26-31 tells of God's standards and true values. Though contrary to man's standards, God uses the common to confuse and confound the world. God may use any of his children to plant churches.

Where should a church be planted? This is the next question that must be decided. There are many ways to find places to start new work. God sometimes works through a Christian living in the community. Sometimes there are no natural leads into a community. God will open the proper door for the interested planter.

Church planting is best done where people are responsive to the gospel. There are some towns that are very difficult because of several factors, the chief being the religion of the people. For example, in a town where there is a strongly dominant religion, it may be very difficult to plant a church. However, outside the town there may be a positive response.

A place where three hundred people are without any kind of church or chapel may be a prospective place for a new church. Often, villages or towns form a somewhat closed unit. They have their own town officials, and the town is marked off with signs showing the boundaries. If there are two small towns joining each other, it may be reasonable to have a church in each town. People will more likely attend a church gathering in their own community than go across the boundary to attend a church in an adjoining community. This suggests the desirability of having a church in every section of a city and in every small community.

Consider a city of sixty thousand people, with more than fifty small communities in that city. Each small community has its own name and identity. How many churches should be planted if the gospel were to be taken in depth to every family? If after intense, long-term witnessing in each community there were a 10 percent harvest, this would be six thousand believers. In order to have an equipping ministry performed in depth with all the members of each family, how many churches would be necessary? The answer to this helps find the answer to the question of where to plant churches. Ten churches is not a correct answer to the problem. Thirty or more perhaps would be a good beginning. The presence of one or two churches in a city of sixty thousand people indicates some serious hang-ups in the ideas of where to plant churches.

A church congregating within walking distance of every person is a good goal in many nations. In densely populated areas churches should be meeting with no more than a kilometer separating them. In high-rise city dwellings there may be need for a church for every block in the city. (Not a church house, but a church.)

Return for a moment to the question of how to find a place to plant a church. First, you go to one place, then another and another. There is no shortcut nor easy substitute for simply getting out among the people. It will be helpful to first get a good map of the area. From government planning agencies facts and figures are available that will give a broad overview of where the people are and what they are doing. From a general study of the area it will be necessary to make a closer study. This may involve a lot of driving and traveling through housing areas. The Lord can use this to make impressions upon a person. Stop and visit with people. Talk to them and give them tracts to read. An unexpected door may open up for church planting. A house-to-house survey will often be helpful in finding a place to get started. It is better to be honest with people. Tell them who you are and what you are doing. Tell them that you are a Bible teacher and that you are available to lead group Bible studies. Somewhere a person will say, "Why don't you come teach us. We are interested."

Once the general area is settled, let the people who are going to make up the study group decide the place of the meeting. If they ask you, the planter, where the meeting should be held, throw it back to them and say, "It is up to you, wherever is best for the group." (In such early decisions as this the people begin to learn to be responsible and make decisions. Remember that part of the goal is a self-governing church. Every action should point toward the fulfillment of a goal—an indigenous church.) They will likely decide to meet in a home.

The country and climate are factors in determining where to

meet. Many Bible study groups have met under a tree, in a public, open meeting place, or in public buildings. A large house of one of the members is often a desired place. It should be within easy reach of as many people as possible. Rather than choose a place on a fringe of a community of one thousand people, it may be best to have meetings in a central location. The planter can drop such hints without being the one to make the decision.

There are advantages to having the meeting at the same place each time. News spreads; people become interested. A regular meeting place reduces confusion.

Under the question of where to plant, the general community has been discussed as well as the specific location in the community. Another dimension of where to plant is important. Church planting is done most effectively among adults. A planter faces the temptation to concentrate on children and youth. These are easier to work with in that they do not pose a threat to the planter. What little child is going to pop up with a theological question that the planter cannot answer? The minds of youth are more pliable and open to new directions than the adults'. It is easier to lead them.

Please understand that this is not a put-down of children's work and Vacation Bible Schools. They are an important ministry of the church. But when the planter has no church, if he wants one he had better concentrate on adults. This depends somewhat on the time that the church planter has. If his only goal is to plant one church in ten years, perhaps it could be done by starting with children. Even if this is possible, is it biblical, and is it the best way? The answer is no. It is not biblical, nor is it the best way.

For example, what happens to the little boy who goes home from the church planter's Bible study and tells his parents that he has been saved? If the parents are zealous followers of some other religion, he may get a beating and certainly no encouragement. He may not be allowed to return to another meeting.

The answer is to win the adults and let them as Christians lead their children to the Lord in the context of a loving church. Adults should be the target for the church planter.

The next question is when to hold the meetings. Again, as much as possible, let this be the decision of the group from the beginning. You can tell them what nights you have open. From that point let the people decide.

There are advantages for having the Bible study on the weekend. This often will be the choice of the people. There are strong advantages in having the Bible study group meet weekly as opposed to nightly. If the people are unsaved and perhaps members of another religion, a gradual, digestible amount of Bible truth is better than a quick overdose which they cannot digest mentally or spiritually. Having a one-hour Bible study one night a week with distribution of take-home reading material allows for thought, study, and an intelligent decision. With five hours of group study five weeks pass, an important amount of time for the Holy Spirit to reach the inner being. This may be likened to the germination of seed. When the seed is planted, conditions make a difference. Time is also a factor. It is unusual to have a harvest immediately after seed is planted in pagan hearts. A degree of germination and cultivation is necessary before harvest is possible.

After the who, where, and when have been decided, one must decide what the seed is to be sown that will most likely bring a harvest—an indigenous church.

The Bible is the most appropriate book for a Bible teacher to teach. (A central task of the church planter is to be a Bible teacher.) The people respect the Bible even if they don't know its contents.

It is obvious that since the seed is to be placed in the lives of unbelievers, the planter would not use seed designed primarily for believers. Paul's letters to the Corinthians were to meet needs of believers, people who were members of the church at Corinth. This portion of the Bible would not be fitting for unbelievers. They would not understand it. Much of the New Testament was written to believers. Parts of Romans and Galatians may benefit unbelievers, even though these Scriptures were written to believers. However, Scriptures written for unbelievers will be more beneficial for a prolonged study by unbelievers.

The purpose of the writing of the Gospel of John was so that people might believe in Jesus and receive life through him (John 20:31). Many church planters use this book to introduce unbelievers to Christ. John's Gospel is a picture of Christ as he makes contact with sinful man for the purpose of redemption. This is where the people are spiritually when the church planter goes to them. This becomes the needed seed to be sown by the planter.

The Gospel of John is available at a low cost. It is usually available in the language of the people. It is one thing to give twenty copies of this booklet to members of a Bible study group. It is quite another thing to give complete Bibles to twenty members. Many church planters cannot finance big Bible giveaways. Even if there is enough money, it is not usually wise to do so. First, people who have never read the Bible will not appreciate it. Also, unless there is personal sacrifice by the reader, the gift will be of less value. The Gospel of John is inexpensive, yet it introduces an unbeliever to Christ. After receiving Christ, a new love for the Bible develops. The new believer then will gladly buy his own Bible.

It is important that from the beginning the planter assure the people that personal philosophy and discussion is of little value unless related to God's Word. The worldwide popularity of the Bible inclines the people to be open to a study of its contents. If a church planter goes to a group and begins a study of set denominational distinctives, he likely will not be received, and perhaps rightfully so. It is wise for the planter to make very clear his immediate objective and the nature and content of the study. Even unbelievers appreciate open honesty.

The seed to be sown is not denominationalism nor personal philosophy. The only appropriate seed is the gospel of Jesus Christ. This gospel (Good News) is most clearly seen in a study of the Gospel of John. The planter must have his Bible, and if possible distribute the Gospel of John booklet to family heads.

Multitudes can plant churches
> Wherever there is a pocket of people
>> Whenever they will receive the Good News.

Note

1. *Missionary Intercom,* October, 1974.

9

How to Employ Indirect Leadership in Church Planting

Broadly speaking, there are two methods of leadership employed in church planting—direct and indirect. Direct leadership is often leader-centered. Indirect leadership centers attention on the group. The spotlight is on the leader in direct leadership, while it is on the group in indirect leadership. Many churches have been planted by church planters using direct leadership methods. This often includes traditional evangelistic crusades. This kind of leadership may have its place in church planting, but because such a critical spotlight beams upon one person, the leader, the number of people capable of such successful leadership is very limited. This kind of leadership requires a special gift in public speaking. It is quickly apparent that many ordinary people would be disqualified. Most will not have the talent to plant churches if strong direct leadership is required.

Mass campaigns using direct leadership methods may complement church planting. The major value of crusades is getting people saved.

Church planting involves this and more. Church planting leads the new converts into a family relationship—an indigenous church. This kind of church is self-governing, self-supporting, and self-propagating. For the leader to bring about the creation of such a church demands a reproducible leadership wherein the members are led to govern, support, and reproduce themselves.

This is best done by indirect leadership. Indirect leadership involves guidance by the leader and participation by the group that will result in rapid transfer of leadership. Guidance, participation, and transfer of leadership become important concepts for the church planter.

The planter should not feel a need to entertain or to hold the group spellbound by his efforts. The outgoing, talkative planter will have to restrain himself if he allows the people to participate. Often the church planter will be so far ahead of the group of unbelievers in biblical knowledge that he faces the subtle temptation to "help" them by telling all he knows on every point.

Perhaps indirect leadership is best seen in an example of actual church planting. The following is a rather detailed example of church planting using indirect methods of leadership. This may be a handle, one way at least, of doing church planting. Every place calls for variation of approach, but it is helpful to have a basic, well-known and tested approach as a guide. Variation then can easily be made to meet particular needs. This method or approach is not *the* approach but *an* approach which is easily reproducible.

From the very beginning the planter should practice principles of indirect leadership. The planter does not make the decision concerning when and where the first Bible study will be held. He guides the people to participate in the decision. Ultimately, the group will make the decision.

The First Meeting—Introduction Night

On the first night the planter takes his Bible, a ball-point pen and a sheet of paper, a sample copy of the Gospel of John, a copy of a fill-in-the-blank study booklet,[1] a small inexpensive songbook or song sheet, one large piece of poster paper with a theme song in bold print, and appropriate tracts. This is all one needs the first night.

The planter, perhaps sitting, introduces himself. He gets to the point of who he is and why he is there. He may say, "I am _____ _____, a Bible teacher from _____." Usually this is enough said. A certain church, an ecclesiastical position, a denomination, is not to be emphasized. More central and crucial to the moment is the fact that the planter is a Bible teacher.

Secondly, the planter introduces his purpose. It is important that he state clearly that his purpose is not to debate, argue, or philosophize. The planter may tell the people that if anyone wishes to debate he is welcome to come to the planter's house at another date for that purpose, but that the meeting time will be used for Bible study. Rarely, if ever, will anyone come. "Philosophizers" must have the crowd to provide an audience to admire their intelligence. It is easier to cut off time-consuming philosophical debate before it begins than after it begins. Then the planter will state the positive purpose of his presence. He may say, "My purpose is to share with you the Good News as found in the Bible, God's Word."

The planter moves into a brief Bible study about a man who came to Jesus. He came seeking the truth, the Good News. His name was Nicodemus. It is not necessary that the planter give a long sermon. Remember, this is an introduction night—an introduction to the planter, his purpose, and the course of study to be pursued. The planter should read John 3:1-18 aloud. What the planter says is not so important. The people do not yet know or trust him. They do respect the Bible, though they do not know its contents. The planter can go back over the story with the people and point out the basic teachings. This story is especially relevant to nominal Christians because they, like Nicodemus, rely upon their physical birth into a religion to make them Christian. This error of Nicodemus is clear in the story, yet he was looking for truth, better news. The story may be concluded with such words as, "Would you like to hear more from God's Word about this Good News, news of a life of peace and joy? How many of you want to continue next week at this same time?" The people indicate their desire to continue by raising their hands. They decide.

Up to this point the planter has used only the Bible. After the people express a desire to continue, the planter shows the books to be studied. He assures the people that the Gospel of John is exactly the same as found in the New Testament. He explains that this is really an introduction to the Bible. The planter states that these are free in a limited number. Later, if the people come to appreciate the Scripture, they can buy a complete Bible. Care must be given to emphasize that the fill-in-the-blank booklet is not Jewish, Catholic, or Protestant. Rather that it is a book with questions and blanks. The answer always will come directly from the Bible—not from the Bible teacher or from the group, but only from the Bible. This puts everybody on even ground with one objective authority—the Bible.

At this stage, it is important to identify the target group for the study. As the Gospel of John and the booklet are being introduced, the planter can tell the group that because of the depth of the study and the nature of the booklet, the study is primarily for adults. Teenagers also are welcome and may participate. Children are welcome to attend, but only adults and teens may receive the study books.

The next items to be used by the planter are the piece of paper and the ball-point pen. Unknown to the unbelievers, a growth-stimulating participation really begins when the planter invites each one to step forward to sign his name and list his age on the paper. The reasons for this signing up are stated to the group before they come forward. The planter states that he wants to know the people better, to learn their names. Second, he wants to know how many Gospels of John and the study booklets to bring next week. There are other reasons for gathering a list of those enrolled, reasons unnecessary to be related to the group. The planter will use this as a weekly attendance check. Each week this list will be used when books are distributed. Names will be called, and the people will claim their books. This will be done for about four weeks. The list will also serve as a permanent record in the file of the planter whether a church is planted or not. This list of names will also indicate to the planter those who have received books.

The next item to be used is the songbook. Since this is introduction night, introduce the idea of learning new gospel songs. If the planter can sing, he may want to sing a song at this point. Then he asks the people if they would like to sing some each week. (The people decide.) Always, the people without hesitation respond positively. The planter then shows the sample copy of the songbook to be used. This should be a songbook in the language of the people. It should be small and inexpensive, with thirty or forty songs.

The next item to be introduced is the theme song. This can be printed on a poster paper folded for convenience. This is held up for the people to see as the planter introduces the theme song. The theme song should give the heart of the gospel message.

The planter thanks the people for coming and invites them to come back the next week for the first Bible study lesson. As the planter bids the people good night, he gives them tracts to take home with them. He will give each adult and teenager a tract. (Do not overgive. It is not bad for family members to share. To have a heavy oversupply may leave an impression that materials are of little value.)

That is the first night, a night of introduction. No more than one hour is needed for this first meeting.

The Second Meeting— Chapter One of the Study Booklet

The planter should take the following items: a Bible, fifteen to twenty copies of the Gospel of John and the fill-in-the-blank booklet, twenty songbooks, twenty-five tracts, and the theme song poster.

Perhaps a word is appropriate concerning the number of books to take. The very nature of this approach will not bring the same kind of crowd as a large, expensive, entertainment-type mass crusade. Often, if a total of fifty adults and teens attend this kind of meeting, only one half will fully participate in filling in the answers in the booklet. Many will come the first night out of curiosity, but may not return. A core of twenty good participants may be an optimum number for this kind of study. Of course, there will be exceptions when the attendance is more. If twenty adults will go all the way through the study, there is a good chance that a nucleus for a new church will come from this group. Twenty songbooks are suggested because this will serve up to fifty adults.

The second meeting will require more patience by the church planter than any other night. This may be more true when the planter seeks to use indirect leadership methods among people who have known only direct, authoritarian leadership. The planter is going to introduce a kind of study that requires individual responsibility and participation. Patience is needed when working with people who have never read a Bible, who do not know a chapter from a verse. This approach demands that they not only find the verse, but also must find the correct answer.

To begin the meeting, the planter greets the group and asks for someone to distribute the songbooks. Every group will vary in its appreciation and aptitude toward music. Some cannot get enough singing while others may not care much for music. A general rule is to sing three songs the first night and add one or more new songs each week. Songs will be repeated. In nine weeks the people can learn at least twenty songs. In two or three weeks the planter should begin transferring music leadership to members of the group. At the third meeting the planter may ask if anyone from the group knows a certain song. (This should be a song learned the previous weeks.) If a hand goes up, the planter invites that person to come lead the song, or at least help him lead it. People will do this if the planter expects them to. Often the natural song leader will emerge before the people are saved. The planter need not appoint a song leader.

After the singing each night the songbooks are collected. Do not permit people to take the books home with them. Let the person who distributes the books know how many there are. This same person will be responsible for collecting the books. It is wise to leave the songbooks in the possession of a responsible person. There is no need for the planter to carry these back to his house every week.

After the songbooks are collected, the planter asks for someone to help him in the distribution of the study booklets. This person comes to the front and calls the names of the enrollees as listed the previous week. As each name is called, the person steps forward to receive his books. A check mark is placed beside his name. (After this meeting the planter will transfer the names of those receiving books to a permanent record sheet prepared to cover eight weeks.)

After each person receives the books, the planter invites any present for the first time to come to the front to enroll. Then the planter again introduces the booklets. He explains that the Gospel of John is a portion of the Bible. He assures the people that this will be the only authority acceptable. He explains the nature of the fill-in-the-blank booklet and how to use it. He will demonstrate by reading the first question and then reading the designated Scripture verse. From this verse he will give the answer. This is the last time the planter will read the question or give the answer in the regular study. He tells the people that they will be the ones to read the questions and find the answers. Everyone is encouraged to participate.

The church planter sits down and relaxes—yet stays in control of the study. Some groups require more direct control than others. The planter invites someone to volunteer to read the first question from the fill-in-the-blank booklet. Someone else volunteers to read the reference verse from the Gospel of John. The reader must wait until everyone has found the verse before he reads. The planter stays alert that no one is left behind. He may need to move among the people on this night to help them learn to locate the verses. After everyone has found it, the verse is read aloud. The planter then may ask the people to find the answer from the verse. Then wait; relax. It sometimes takes awhile for unbelievers to find the answer; but they will. Let a volunteer state the answer for the group. The people will write the answer in the blank. Watch the pens. When all have finished writing, the planter will ask someone to read the next question. Until the people catch on and feel relaxed, there may be moments of hesitation and silence. The planter can still relax and wait. He will move at the pace of the people.

There is no need for the planter to sermonize on every point. Let the Scripture speak for itself. Remember that the planter has promised the group that the only totally acceptable authority is God's Word. The booklet is asking relevant questions, and the answers come directly from the Bible. There are times for the planter to add his comments but not necessarily on every point.

At the end of the lesson it may be helpful if the planter reads through all the lesson with the blanks filled in. This will serve as a review to drive the lesson home deeper in the minds of the people. It will also help anyone who missed one or two blanks. As the planter reads straight through the lesson, this person can fill in the blanks.

After reading the lesson, the planter will say, "Are there any questions concerning the lesson that we have studied tonight?" Until the planter knows his group, this narrowing down of the scope of the discussion is important. Simply to ask, "Do you have any questions?" opens the door to debaters or people who will take much time on questions that are not relevant for the unbelievers in the group.

If there are no questions the planter tells the people to put their names on their books and then pass them to the front. The books will be kept by a responsible person in the group until the next meeting when they will again be given out. If the people take the books home with them after the first night of use, many of the books will be lost, or some of the people will not return. The first two or three meetings attract serious students and curious students. The serious remain, but many of the curious will drop out. It is best to take up the books for at least the first three or four weeks. Beyond this time the planter will know those who are genuinely interested. They, then, may take their books home after each meeting.

The crowds usually will decrease in number after three weeks. Some will drop out after they see that it is simply the gospel being presented. In some cultures peer and family pressure may influence some to drop out.

After lesson one the people feel freer to participate and have more understanding of how to use the materials. This makes it easier to move through the next lessons. The procedure is the same throughout the booklet. Tracts should be distributed following each lesson.

The Seventh Meeting — Chapter Six in the Study Booklet

Another stage develops at about the seventh week. The entire study booklet should deal with how to find the abundant life. After about six weeks the truth gets close to the believer, making him aware of his need. The tract that is given following the sixth week is crucial. The unbelievers will have this tract to supplement their regular study. Six weeks of Bible study will usually prepare the people to make an intelligent decision. The study booklet will guide the people to the point of decision.

Normally, in an area where another religion is very dominant and deep-seated, it will take at least seven weeks for people to make a decision based upon adequate knowledge. This is also true where people are ignorant of basic biblical truths. Of course, there is nothing magical in the seventh week, but time is a factor if churches are to be planted with regenerate members as the base.

When the Holy Spirit opens the door for the invitation to be given to the people to make their decisions, the planter must take time to see that everyone understands what he is doing. Every seeker should pray a sinner's prayer. Following the decisions, counseling, and prayer, the planter should lead the members to pray their first prayers as new Christians. If there are few or many new believers, urge each one to pray a short prayer of thanksgiving. This is the beginning of a natural participation in the life of the future church.

The Eighth Meeting— Chapter Seven in the Study Booklet

Following week number seven, or the big week of decision, the group studies the final chapter in the study booklet. This chapter reviews the key points of the first six chapters and leads up to another throwing out of the net to catch those yet lost.

At this point some of the people have been saved for more than a week. By now the planter is only introducing new songs while one or more of the group have taken over the leading of the singing. Special music is a regular feature from the group.

At this time the people make another decision. The study booklet is completed. What next? The planter will ask if they want to continue. If the answer is positive the planter is free to make a suggestion about the next study. He will recommend another booklet concerning basic Bible doctrines and the Christian life. Its format will probably be different from the first fill-in-the-blank booklet. The planter introduces the booklet and encourages each family to buy one. These booklets are about the price of a soft drink in most countries so are within the means of everyone.

A major change comes at this point. The planter asks the group to choose one of the new believers to lead in a discussion of the first chapter of the new study booklet on the following week. The decision is for the people to make. They may have one person to lead the study through several chapters, or they may ask a different person to lead each week. The church planter himself should not lead the study.

The Ninth Meeting—Beginning a New Study

The church planter attends as one of the group to listen as the new believers lead the singing and the study. It may be necessary for the planter to give a few hints to the song leader and study leader, but he does not need to tell them every step to take. He may tell the study leader that he is to use any method possible to help all the people to fully understand the lesson in the booklet. Then if he wants to read it, preach it, or discuss it, it is up to him and God. The group will continue this study for approximately two months. The church planter will find reasons for missing a few of these meetings. When he does not come, the study goes on.

Indirect leadership in this chapter means a low-profile guidance by the church planter in leading a participating group toward a preconceived goal.

In conclusion, a word is in order concerning the study booklet to be used for the first two months.

The use of this booklet is valuable because:

1. It is reproducible. A high level of education is not necessary. A member of the new church can go to another place and plant another church even if he is not a polished speaker.

2. The use of the booklet serves as a guide to keep the study going in the right direction. It helps to cut off undesirable philosophical debate.

3. It provides the people a helpful visual aid tool to make group participation natural and easy.

4. When finished, the people have something for personal reference or something to be used in helping others, or even to teach to another group with the aim of planting a church.

This is one way of planting churches. Adaptation will be necessary from place to place. The Lord will give wisdom in every situation. He is the planter's primary and ultimate guide in the technique employed.

Note

1. Any church planter could write such a booklet to meet the particular needs of the people with whom he is working. The booklet should bring people to a clear understanding of sin, repentance, forgiveness, and authentic faith. If the Gospel of John portion is used, all answers should be found in that Gospel. Any other Scripture references should be printed in the booklet.

10

From a Bible Study Group to a Church

The Bible study group as discussed in this book is different from the traditional home Bible study in a home or extension Bible class. It is different in the number of people involved and often different in the chosen location of the meetings. A Bible study in a home focuses more on a home with a few neighbors invited. The Bible study group focuses on a community, a sizable pocket of people. The purpose is often different. A church may sponsor a Bible study for many months without thought of the birth of a new church. The primary function of the Bible study or extension class usually is as an arm of the "mother church." There are legitimate needs for such classes. These need to be seen as what they are and not as church planting efforts. Some, in order to swing with the times, begin to call Bible studies by an abused term, house church, even though the idea of an indigenous church is never anticipated.

The new church will not be a house church. The churches that met in houses in the New Testament were not called house churches; they were called churches. The place of the meeting made them no more or no less a church. The place where the Bible study group meets is not a determining factor in the development of that group into a church. The new church may continue to meet where the Bible study group met before. It may be in a house, a public building, school house, rented quarters, or eventually in a chapel constructed by the members.

Some may ask how many members are necessary to organize a church. There is no number given in the New Testament concerning this. Two or three people could be a church. The proven quality rather than large quantity determines when a Bible study group should become a church. In many cultures it is better if the church can be born with at least ten adult members. In face of persecution and hardships this number would provide needed encouragement. But a church can be a true church with fewer than ten members.

From the beginning of the Bible study group, the planter has definite objectives in mind. His immediate objective is the salvation of a core of people who will bring about the intermediate objective—the planting of an indigenous church. Because of definite planning and procedure the movement from a Bible study group is not accidental nor haphazard. Just as a strategy is helpful in leading the people to a responsible decision to accept Christ, so must the planter plan for a graduation from a Bible study group to a church. This is a move anticipated by the planter from the beginning. Usually, because an unbelieving mind could not comprehend the intermediate step—a church—before reaching the immediate step—salvation—it is not helpful for the planter to disclose his intermediate and ultimate objectives at the beginning of the Bible study group. On the night of introduction he need not say that he plans to plant a church.

A key to development toward an indigenous church is the planter's willingness to share responsibilities with group members. If the church planter must have someone who can preach as he can before he allows one from the group to try, the planter becomes a major obstacle in planting an indigenous church.

If the approach given in the last chapter is followed, a church may be born between ten to fifteen weeks from the night of the planter's introduction. After the completion of a study that has led the group members to salvation, they begin a study of a book that introduces them to the life of the Christian. This book takes up where the first study booklet ended. The purpose of this second book is to lead the group into a church family relationship with all its privileges and responsibilities. The study will be led by group members. The planter's presence will be keenly felt, though he will not lead. He will give extra time as may be necessary in discussing all the topics, especially baptism and the church.

There are basic requirements to be met for the Bible study group to become a church. The first requirement is that the people be truly converted to Christ and his way of living. Previous to baptism and the formation of a new church family, every candidate for membership should demonstrate a changed life. The second requirement is New Testament baptism. It is only fair that the planter tell the people what they are getting into before they are baptized and become members of a new fellowship called a church. The life of the church, its privileges and responsibilities, should be openly discussed. No one should be scared away intentionally, but those who are not serious should not enter.

These requirements, conversion, believer's baptism, and an acceptable understanding of the nature of the church, are the basics to be met in order for a church to be born.

When the planter discusses the nature of the church, he will talk about the three principles of an indigenous church. Technically, it is unlikely that a church will be fully indigenous when it is born. But there should be a large degree of self-government, self-support, and self-propagation at the time of birth. These are some basic characteristics of life itself in a church. Self-support is not a problem. Any church can support itself financially at its particular stage of growth and need. Though not the dominant, final voice, the planter can continue to encourage and give occasional direction to the young church related to the governing of itself and to its propagation of the gospel. He can and often should give special instruction on basic doctrines, etc.

A Bible study group becomes a church when people dead in sin become, through faith in Jesus Christ, a living organism characterized by a Christ-sustained ability to govern, support, and propagate itself. The act of baptism is the mark of allegiance to Christ and of a special church family relationship.

The planter likely will be the one to baptize the first new converts. The next time there are candidates for baptism, he should do no more than assist the new church leader. The third time, the planter should be an observer. (A church member so designated by the church can baptize, even if he has not been ordained by man.)

After the new believers have been baptized, the planter should meet with them to discuss the future life of the church. Adequate time needs to be given to discuss the qualifications and the role of the pastor. The planter can point the members to Scripture passages that will help them understand the work of the pastor. In the meantime, it may be healthy for the church to choose from the membership someone to be the Bible teacher. It is better to have a time of testing and an opportunity to gain experience and understanding before the person is recognized as pastor. Much prayer should precede the church's choice of the Bible teacher. After the person chosen as Bible teacher has served for a few months, perhaps the church and the teacher will feel certain of God's ordination of that person for the task of pastoring. Then, with or without ceremony and announcement, the Bible teacher begins to function as their pastor.

The church will officially recognize one of the members as the regular song leader. Perhaps a secretary and treasurer will be elected at this time. The church will decide when the members will gather for worship. The church planter can afford to let the people make these decisions. Once the time is set, the planter can give a few hints concerning the worship program. He need not give an order of service which must be followed. It is best to give general instructions at this point and let the people be creative. The planter should tell the people that worship includes prayer, singing, and Bible study. The order and the length of time for each of these should be flexible to meet the needs of the people. This is the beginning. Maybe the first worship program will not include "passing the plate," but this will come as the people practice the other three aspects of worship. They usually will see the need of offerings very early in the life of the church.

The worship program should be simple and should evolve naturally out of creative, Spirit-led minds. Hopefully, the church will gather on Sunday for worship, but the planter should not tell the people they must meet for Sunday School at 9:45 AM and for worship at 11:00 AM, with Wednesday prayer meeting at 7:30 PM. The straitjacket of time will come soon enough. At least let the church design its own jacket.

After the church chooses the Bible teacher, song leader, and other necessary officers, training must be provided. The planter can easily and quickly give helpful ideas to the song leader, secretary, and treasurer. More time is needed to help the Bible teacher who will likely become the pastor.

It is amazing what a God-called man can do in a few weeks. In order for the church to be fed, the planter will guide the new leader toward biblical exposition. After the organizational meeting, the planter assumes that the total program will be led by the chosen leaders. The song leader or someone else may be the emcee, and the Bible teacher will teach the lesson. The planter may tell the teacher to prayerfully select a passage of Scripture that will help the people. The teacher should read the passage many times, take notes, write down outstanding truths, and listen to what God is saying. Then at the next service he will read the Scripture to the people and tell them as clearly as possible what God wants them to know. God will use such a sincere, called man, even with this little instruction from the planter.

There are other helpful pointers which the planter can give the new teacher.

1. Strongly encourage the leader to involve every member in various ways and especially in prayer. There is something wrong with the leader or pastor who does more than 50 percent of the public praying. Noninvolvement by the congregation results in spiritual paralysis. The leader will sometimes need to personally encourage and teach people to pray publicly.

2. The leader should permit the song leader to be in charge of the music. The song leader should work with the teacher to better harmonize the total program. Sometimes, if the leader is a natural, gifted speaker, he may desire to talk when perhaps someone of less speaking ability should be talking.

3. Many times someone other than the Bible teacher or song leader should be the emcee of the worship service.

4. If the Bible teacher is mature, he will tolerate an assistant. The teacher may have full secular employment, plus he now has a new, demanding task as teacher/pastor. An assistant can give relief to the teacher and at the same time increase the number doing a valuable ministry.

In-depth training must be provided for the new leader. If no one else is available, the church planter should provide special classes for new leaders. He can work this into his schedule while planting churches in other nearby areas. Basic in this training is an introduction to the Bible, witnessing, the work of the pastor, and preaching preliminaries. If possible, one half-day each week should be given to these studies. The new church will provide the finances necessary for books and the personal expenses of the leader. This special training should last for at least three months. Then, if some sort of extension theological training is available, most pastors can enroll in a continuous leadership training program, yet care for their families and pastor the church. If the pastor learns early that he is only one of many ministers in the church, his load will be less burdensome and frustrating. He is to minister to ministers in order that they might do the work of the ministry. Whatever the degree of his training, this concept is central.

With this degree of training and proficiency, the church has a leader who is not a layman. He has specialized training for particular tasks. With continued training, fellowship with other church leaders, and the prayers of the members, the Bible teacher can develop into a powerful preacher and effective pastor under God. The answer is to begin and end with God.

11

Church Planting Unhindered

There will be struggles, pain, and hardships in the birth of churches, but victory is possible because the concept was born in the mind of God. In spite of the barnacles of tradition, fresh New Testament churches continue to be born. In a time when many denominations are substituting social service for Christian expansion, and still others are convinced that missions and missionaries are dated, churches continue to be born. The challenging promise of Jesus is as relevant today as it was in New Testament days. He said, "I will build my church, and not even death will ever be able to overcome it" (Matt. 16:18b, TEV).

Satan is fighting day and night against New Testament church expansion. There will always be opposition. Jesus recognized this, but he was confident of victory. As long as the planters realize that it is his church, and it is he who is the builder, the birth of churches will go on unhindered.

Frank Stagg rightfully uses this term *unhindered* in his work, *The Book of Acts*. The term is used to describe the spread of churches in the first-century pagan society. Today's world is just as pagan. The answer is no less than it was in Paul's day—the establishment, or the planting, of indigenous churches. The planting of such churches is a key part of God's plan of redemption for mankind.

96 INDIGENOUS CHURCH PLANTING

In the power of the Holy Spirit, Bible believers have no other alternative than to scale the barriers, narrow the limitations, and move in step with God in pushing back the frontiers of paganism, by the rapid establishment of indigenous churches.

LINCOLN CHRISTIAN COLLEGE AND SEMINARY